from THE KENNEDY WIT:

"When we got into office, the thing that surprised me most was to find that things were just as bad as we'd been saying they were."

* * *

"I see nothing wrong with giving Robert some legal experience as Attorney General before he goes out to practice law."

* * *

"I do not think it entirely inappropriate to introduce myself to this audience. I am the man who accompanied Jacqueline Kennedy to Paris, and I have enjoyed it."

* * *

LITTLE BOY: "Mr. President, how did you become a war hero?"

PRESIDENT KENNEDY: "It was absolutely involuntary. They sank my boat."

All the warmth, wit, humor, and charm of JFK himself, gathered from his campaign speeches, "off the cuff" remarks, press conferences and prepared addresses . . . from his first days as a public speaker to his words as Senator and President.

THE
KENNEDY
WIT

THE
KENNEDY
WIT

Edited by
BILL ADLER

*This low-priced Bantam Book
has been completely reset in a type face
designed for easy reading, and was printed
from new plates. It contains the complete
text of the original hard-cover edition.*
NOT ONE WORD HAS BEEN OMITTED.

THE KENNEDY WIT

*A Bantam Book / published by arrangement with
The Citadel Press*

PRINTING HISTORY

*Citadel edition published July 1964
2nd printing July 1964
3rd printing July 1964
4th printing August 1964
5th printing September 1964
6th printing October 1964
Bantam edition published February 1965*

PHOTOGRAPHS COURTESY WIDE WORLD PHOTOS
AND UNITED PRESS INTERNATIONAL

*Bantam Books are published by Bantam Books, Inc., a subsidiary
of Grosset & Dunlap, Inc. Its trade-mark, consisting of the words
"Bantam Books" and the portrayal of a bantam, is registered in the
United States Patent Office and in other countries. Marca Registrada.
Bantam Books, Inc., 271 Madison Avenue, New York 16, New York.*

PRINTED IN THE UNITED STATES OF AMERICA

CONTENTS

THE
KENNEDY
WIT

THE
KENNEDY
WIT

John F. Kennedy was a man with a keenly developed sense of humor. Few men in public life have displayed such wit in their speeches and writings.

Unquestionably, a great sense of humor is a blessing for the President of the United States, for no job in the world is more fraught with the continual pressure of important decisions. Surely, John F. Kennedy's unique wit enabled him to live through many tense hours with greater ease.

It has been said that nothing describes a man better than his own sense of humor. I think that you will find this to be true of President Kennedy.

From the material in this book, you will draw a new picture of John F. Kennedy and that delightful facet of his personality. From his penetrating wit that developed during the hectic days of the campaign to the engaging humor he showed as President, a new portrait of John F. Kennedy emerges.

Bill Adler
New York City
April, 1964

THE 1960 CAMPAIGN

THE 1960 CAMPAIGN

I know something about Mr. Khrushchev, whom I met a year ago in the Senate Foreign Relations Committee, and I know something about the nature and history of his country, which I visited in 1939.

Mr. Khrushchev himself, it is said, told the story a few years ago about the Russian who began to run through the Kremlin, shouting, 'Khrushchev is a fool. Khrushchev is a fool.' He was sentenced, the Premier said, to twenty-three years in prison, 'three for insulting the party secretary, and twenty for revealing a state secret.'

Pikesville, Maryland
September 16, 1960

Someone was kind enough, though I don't know whether he meant it kindly, to say the other night that in my campaign in California I sounded like a Truman with a Harvard accent.

New York City
September 14, 1960

Ladies and gentlemen, I was warned to be out here in plenty of time to permit those who are going to the Green Bay Packers game to leave. I don't mind running against Mr. Nixon but I have the good sense not to run against the Green Bay Packers.

> Green Bay, Wisconsin
> October, 1960

During the campaign, there was only one occasion in which candidate Kennedy and candidate Nixon appeared at the same dinner. It occurred at the Alfred Smith Memorial Dinner at the Waldorf-Astoria Hotel in New York. These were Mr. Kennedy's opening remarks:

I am glad to be here at this notable dinner once again, and I am glad that Mr. Nixon is here, also. Now that Cardinal Spellman has demonstrated the proper spirit, I assume that shortly I will be invited to a Quaker dinner honoring Herbert Hoover.

Cardinal Spellman is the only man so widely respected in American politics that he could bring together, amicably, at the same banquet table, for the first time in this campaign, two political leaders who are increasingly apprehensive about the November election, who have long eyed each other suspiciously, and who have disagreed so strongly, both publicly and privately—Vice President Nixon and Governor Rockefeller.

Mr. Nixon, like the rest of us, has had his troubles in this campaign. At one point even the *Wall Street Journal* was criticizing his tactics. That is like the *Osservatore Romano* criticizing the Pope.

One of the inspiring notes that was struck in the

last debate was struck by the Vice President in his very moving warning to the candidates against the use of profanity by Presidents and ex-Presidents when they are on the stump. And I know after fourteen years in the Congress with the Vice President, that he was very sincere in his views about the use of profanity. But I am told that a prominent Republican said to him yesterday in Jacksonville, Florida, "Mr. Vice President, that was a damn fine speech." And the Vice President said, "I appreciate the compliment but not the language." And the Republican went on, "Yes, sir, I liked it so much that I contributed a thousand dollars to your campaign." And Mr. Nixon replied, "The hell you say."

However, I would not want to give the impression that I am taking former President Truman's use of language lightly. I have sent him the following wire:

"Dear Mr. President: I have noted with interest your suggestion as to where those who vote for my opponent should go. While I understand and sympathize with your deep motivation, I think it is important that our side try to refrain from raising the religious issue."

Alfred Smith Memorial Dinner
New York City
October 19, 1960

How can any farmer vote Republican in 1960? I understand nearby there was a farmer who planted some corn. He said to his neighbor, "I hope I break even this year. I really need the money."

Grand View, Missouri
October 22, 1960

The Vice President has claimed Al Smith for his work in his later years and I claimed him for his work in the 1928 campaign. Neither one of us indicated what Al Smith would do in 1960. It is possible he would have *voted* Republican, but I think he would have *prayed* Democratic this year.

> *New York City*
> *October 20, 1960*

Raising funds during a political campaign is an essential part of our political system. During the Presidential campaign, Mr. Kennedy spoke before many $100-a-plate dinners and, on occasion, referred to the cost of these affairs with these remarks:

I am deeply touched—not as deeply touched as you have been by coming to this dinner, but nevertheless, it is a sentimental occasion.

> *Fund-Raising Dinner*
> *Salt Lake City, Utah*
> *September 23, 1960*

We had an interesting convention at Los Angeles and we ended with a strong Democratic platform which we called "The Rights of Man." The Republican platform has also been presented. I do not know its title, but it has been referred to as "The Power of Positive Thinking."

> *New York City*
> *September 14, 1960*

I have been informed that with this dinner I am now responsible as the leader of the Democratic Party for a debt of over one million dollars. I don't know—they spend it like they were sure we were going to win.

There is a story about a Texan who went to New York and told a New Yorker that he could jump off the Empire State Building and live. The Easterner said, "Well, that would be an accident." He said, "Suppose I did it twice?" The Easterner said, "That would be an accident, too." "Suppose I did it three times?" And the Easterner said, "That would be a habit."

Texas twice, in 1952 and 1956, jumped off the Democratic band wagon. We are down here to see it is not going to be a habit.

El Paso, Texas
September 12, 1960

I wonder when he [Mr. Nixon] put his finger under Mr. Khrushchev's nose whether he was saying, "I know you are ahead of us in rockets, Mr. Khrushchev, but we are ahead of you in color television." I would just as soon look at black and white television and be ahead of them in rockets.

Pittsburgh, Pennsylvania
October 10, 1960

I'm glad to be here because I feel a sense of kinship with the Pittsburgh Pirates. Like my candidacy, they were not given much chance in the spring.

Harrisburg, Pennsylvania
September, 1960

President Truman told me the other night that his campaign train ran out of funds three times in 1948 and they had to come and get him. We are trying to keep going.

Charleston, West Virginia
September 19, 1960

I don't see how the Flint High School football team ever loses any football game with that cheering section. If they are not busy for the next two months in school, we will be glad to take them with us all around the United States.

Flint, Michigan
September 5, 1960

I want to express my regrets for being late. They told me five days ago a storm was coming up here, so we waited.

Columbia, South Carolina
October 10, 1960

In a speech on the University of Illinois campus, Mr. Kennedy made reference to his famous television debates with Mr. Nixon in this remark:

A good deal of comparison, and most of it unfavorable, is drawn between the Lincoln-Douglas debates and my weekly brief appearance on "What's Our Line?" every Friday night.

October 24, 1960

Question: Senator, you were promised military intelligence briefing from the President. Have you received that?

Mr. Kennedy: Yes. I talked on Thursday morning to General Wheeler from the Defense Department.

Question: What was his first name?

Mr. Kennedy: He didn't brief me on that.

Press Conference
Anchorage, Alaska
September 4, 1960

This week I had the opportunity to debate with Mr. Nixon. I feel that I should reveal that I had a great advantage in that debate and I am not referring to anyone's makeup man. The advantage that I had was that Mr. Nixon had just debated with Khrushchev and I had debated with Hubert Humphrey and that gave me an edge.

Minneapolis, Minnesota
October 1, 1960

I know that there are some Americans and some Democrats who say that they have now developed a wonderful arrangement in Washington. The Congress is Democratic and the President is Republican and nothing happens and isn't it wonderful?

Alexandria, Virginia
August 24, 1960

Much was said during the campaign about the relative experience of Mr. Kennedy and Mr. Nixon. On this point, Mr. Kennedy made these remarks in a speech in Jacksonville, Florida in October, 1960:

I know a banker who served thirty years as president of a bank. He had more experience, until his bank went broke, than any other banker in Massachusetts. But if I ever go in the banking business, I do not plan to hire him, and he knows the operation from top to bottom.

It is, I think, a source of concern to us all that the first dogs carried around in outer space were not named Rover and Fido but instead were named Belka and Strelka. It was not named Checkers,* either.

Muskegon, Michigan
September 5, 1960

I want to thank that band. One more chorus of "Anchors Aweigh" and we will just float this building right out.

Akron, Ohio
September, 1960

One of the major Republican campaign issues was that Mr. Kennedy lacked the experience necessary for the Presidency. Mr. Kennedy had this to say about that issue in a political speech in Minneapolis in October, 1960.

Ladies and gentlemen, the outstanding news story of this week was not the events of the United Nations or even the Presidential campaign. It was a story coming out of my own city of Boston that Ted Williams of the Boston Red Sox had retired from baseball. It seems that at forty-two he was too old. It shows that perhaps experience isn't enough.

The Republicans have run in this century, Mr. McKinley, Harding—do you know what his slogan was? "Return to Normalcy." "Keep Cool with Coolidge," "A Chicken in Every Pot" with Herbert Hoover. I don't know what Dewey's slogan was because we never really found out.

Wilkes-Barre, Pennsylvania
October, 1960

I was informed when I started out this morning that we were going to travel in Delaware County, which voted 8 to 1 for Alf Landon. We are going to wipe that record out. No county in the United States should have that reputation.

Norristown, Pennsylvania
October 29, 1960

First, we will not rely on a monetary policy that puts its emphasis on tight money and high interest rates. The fact of the matter is, as Frank Church said in his keynote speech, if Rip Van Winkle went to sleep and he woke up and he wanted to know whether the Republicans or the Democrats were in office, he would just say, "How high are the interest rates?"

Saginaw, Michigan
October 14, 1960

I do not want it said of our generation what T. S. Eliot wrote in his poem, "The Rock"—"and the wind shall say: 'these were decent people, their only monument the asphalt road and a thousand lost golf balls.'" We can do better than that.

Columbus, Ohio
October 17, 1960

This isn't the way they told me it was when I first decided to run for the Presidency. After reading about the schedules of the President, I thought we all stayed in bed until ten or eleven and then got out and drove around.

Rockford, Illinois
October 24, 1960

Prior to the nomination of Lyndon Johnson as the Democratic Vice Presidential candidate, there were rumors that Governor Pat Brown of California was interested in the nomination. This presented problems for Mr. Kennedy, because Governor Brown is also a Catholic. And, needless to say, two Catholics running on the same ticket certainly was not a balanced ticket. In a speech in California, prior to the convention, Mr. Kennedy had this to say about Governor Brown:

I know there has been talk out here about a Kennedy-Brown ticket, and I sincerely wish that we could arrange that. Unfortunately, I come from Massachusetts and the Governor comes from California, and I don't believe the country is ready for a ticket that stretches from the Atlantic to the Pacific.

I appreciate your welcome. As the cow said to the Maine farmer, "Thank you for a warm hand on a cold morning."

Los Angeles, California
November 2, 1960

I want to express my great appreciation to all of you for your kindness in coming out and giving us a warm Hoosier welcome. I understand that this town suffered a misfortune this morning when the bank was robbed. I am confident that the *Indianapolis Star* will say "Democrats Arrive and Bank Robbed." But we don't believe that.

Anderson, Indiana
October 5, 1960

I come to Suffolk County and ask your help. If we can do well in this county, and I ask your help in doing well, we're going to put this speech to music and make a fortune out of it.

Commack, Long Island, New York
November 6, 1960

One of the problems of a political campaign is that the candidate must be prepared to make a political speech at any time of day. President Kennedy referred to this problem in a speech in Anchorage, Alaska in September, 1960.

I want to express my appreciation for that warm Alaskan welcome. As Bob Bartlett said, we started out about nine o'clock in the morning from Baltimore and it is now four o'clock in the morning for those of us living on Eastern time. I have not made a speech that late in the evening since some of the early Massachusetts political banquets which I attended when I was first a Congressman, when they would put the junior members on about this hour.

During the campaign, Kennedy often remarked about the long and tough role of campaigning. He made these remarks on that subject in a speech in Dayton, Ohio, October 17, 1960:

Franklin Roosevelt started his campaign here in Ohio. I don't know what has happened to politics, but whenever I read about the 1932 campaign, Franklin Roosevelt stayed in Albany all winter, spring, summer, didn't go to the convention until he was nominated. He then took a boating trip up the coast of Maine with his son, started his campaign late in September, made some speeches, and was elected by a tremendous majority.

I personally have lived through ten Presidential campaigns, but I must say the eleventh makes me feel like I lived through twenty-five.

New York City
September 14, 1960

Ladies and gentlemen, the devices which are used in the City of New York to separate you from your life savings are numerous. When the dinners run out, the luncheons begin, and when the luncheons run out, the breakfasts begin. We may all meet next week to get the campaign out of the red with a midnight brunch at eighty-five dollars a person—and I will be there.

New York City
November 5, 1960

I want to express my appreciation to the Governor. Every time he introduces me as the potentially greatest President in the history of the United States, I always think perhaps he is overstating it one or two degrees. George Washington wasn't a bad President and I do want to say a word for Thomas Jefferson. But, otherwise, I will accept the compliment.

Muskegon, Michigan
September 5, 1960

Ladies and gentlemen, it is my understanding that the last candidate for the Presidency to visit this community in a presidential year was Herbert Hoover in 1928.

President Hoover initiated on the occasion of his visit the slogan "Two chickens for every pot," and it is no accident that no Presidential candidate has ever dared come back to this community since.

Bristol, Tennessee
September 21, 1960

Question: Senator, Governor Pat Brown today issued a very optimistic statement. Yet a poll shows Nixon running ahead. Which of these two experts do you believe?

Mr. Kennedy: I believe Governor Brown.

Burbank, California
September 9, 1960

I come from a non-agricultural state, Massachusetts, and, therefore, I am sure that there are some farmers in Iowa and South Dakota who say, "Why should we elect someone from New England? Why shouldn't we elect a farmer?" Well, there is no farmer up for the office this year. Whittier, California,* is not one of the great agricultural sections of the United States.

Sioux City, Iowa
September 21, 1960

Ladies and gentlemen, I want to express my appreciation to all of you for being kind enough to wait at the airport for my sister and myself, and also my regrets for being so late. In case any of you wanted to run for the Presidency, I would say we started this morning in Iowa, we spoke in South Dakota, we speak now in North Dakota, we speak at a dinner meeting in Montana, and end up in Wyoming tonight. I think that my election chief thinks that the election is October 8 rather than November 8.

Fargo, North Dakota
September 22, 1960

Last week a noted clergyman was quoted as saying that our society may survive in the event of my election but it certainly won't be what it was. I would like to think he was complimenting me, but I'm not sure he was.

New York City
September 14, 1960

I want to express my thanks to all of you, particularly those of you who are college students and can't vote, who came down here anyway. I recognize that the sacrifice is not extensive as I am doing the work this morning and you are not in class. I am glad that you are participating actively in the political process. Artemus Ward, fifty years ago, said, "I am not a politician and my other habits are also good."

Albion, Michigan
October 14, 1960

Question: Senator, when does the moratorium end on Nixon's hospitalization and your ability to attack him?

Mr. Kennedy: Well, I said I would not mention him unless I could praise him until he got out of the hospital, and I have not mentioned him.

Burbank, California
September 9, 1960

Texas has sent twenty-one Democratic Congressmen to Congress and one Republican, a fair proportion, a good average.

El Paso, Texas
September 12, 1960

We don't want to be like the leader in the French Revolution who said, "There go my people. I must find out where they are going so I can lead them."

I regret the rain, but it rains, as the Bible tells us, on the just and the unjust alike, on Republicans as well as Democrats.

Sioux Falls, South Dakota
September 22, 1960

When I came to Washington to the U.S. Senate, I brought a number of young ladies from Massachusetts to be secretaries. They all got married. Then I got a whole new set of girls and they got married. So if any of you girls feel the prospects are limited in this community you come and work for me.

Those of you who live in this State of Florida depend upon a moving and expanding country. I know something about the economy of this State. When the rest of the country catches cold, Florida gets pneumonia and Miami is very sick.

Miami, Florida
October 18, 1960

This state knows the issues of this campaign—Senior Citizens. Senator McNamara is chairman of the Senate Committee on Senior Citizens. I am vice chairman. We are both aging fast.

Warren, Michigan
October 26, 1960

You remember the very old story about a citizen of Boston who heard a Texan talking about the glories of Bowie, Davy Crockett, and all the rest, and finally said, "Haven't you heard of Paul Revere?" To which the Texan answered, "Well, he is the man who ran for help."

Houston, Texas
September 12, 1960

The man in the audience said that I should tell Mr. Nixon that experience is what he will have left after this campaign is over. I don't know why we never think of these things.

First, let me say that you are my type of Democrat. My friends, Bob Wagner, General Farley, Frank O'Connor, Pat Clancy—the Irish are very big out here. Jim Delaney—they really run a balanced ticket.

New York City
October 27, 1960

THE PRESIDENCY

Comments by President Kennedy at Inaugural Balls:

I think this is an ideal way to spend an evening and I hope that we can all meet here again tomorrow at one A.M. to do it all over again.

I don't know a better way to spend an evening— you looking at us and we looking at you.

The Johnsons and I have been to five balls tonight, and we still have one unfulfilled ambition—and that is to see somebody dance.

Washington, D. C.
January 20, 1961

On a trip to the West Coast, President Kennedy was asked by a little boy, "Mr. President, how did you become a war hero?"

It was absolutely involuntary. They sank my boat.

On a state visit to France, President Kennedy attended the Paris ballet one night, as guest of President Charles de Gaulle. During the intermission, the Kennedys and their host retired to a theatre anteroom. French photographers were let in, for a quick historical portrait, then dismissed with an imperious flick of a de Gaulle finger. "Don't you wish you could control your photographers like that?" a reporter asked Mr. Kennedy. President Kennedy remarked dryly:

You must remember that I wasn't recalled to office as *my* country's savior.

June 1, 1961

I suppose a number of things attract us all here today. Some of us think it wise to associate as much as possible with historians and cultivate their good will, though we always have the remedy which Winston Churchill once suggested when he prophesied during World War II that history would deal gently with us. "Because," Mr. Churchill said, "I intend to write it!"

Washington, D. C.
October 3, 1961

During his meeting with Premier Khrushchev in Vienna, President Kennedy noticed a medal on Khrushchev's chest and asked what it was. The Premier replied that the medal was the Lenin Peace Prize.

"I hope you keep it," Mr. Kennedy commented.

In a tribute to Senator Warren Magnuson of Washington, President Kennedy listed Magnuson's Senate techniques:

He never visits the Senate until late in the afternoon, when almost everybody has gone home. He comes in at the last minute and waits until he can have the floor, and then he says, "What's my business? Oh, it's nothing important. Just the Grand Coulee Dam!"

At a Democratic fund raising dinner in Miami honoring Senator George A. Smathers of Florida, President Kennedy made these remarks:

Senator Smathers has been one of my most valuable counselors at crucial moments. In 1952 when I was thinking of running for the United States Senate, I went to Senator Smathers and said, "George, what do you think?" He said, "Don't do it, can't win, bad year." [*That was the year Mr. Kennedy won his Senate seat.*]

In 1956, I didn't know whether I should run for vice president or not so I said, "George, what do you think?" And Senator Smathers replied, "It's your choice!" So I ran and lost.

In 1960 I was wondering whether I ought to run in the West Virginia primary, but the Senator said, "Don't do it. That state you can't possibly carry."

And actually, the only time I really got nervous about the whole matter of Los Angeles was just before the balloting and George came up and said, "I think it looks pretty good for you."

March 11, 1962

President Kennedy played host to President Aub Khan of Pakistan at Mount Vernon. Secretary of the Interior Udall was chatting with President Aub's daughter and told her that he had once climbed a certain mountain in Pakistan. Unfortunately, Secretary Udall was mistaken; the mountain that he was referring to happened to be in neighboring Afghanistan and was hotly disputed. President Kennedy happened to overhear the Secretary's mistake and saved the situation by saying:

Madam, that is why I named Mr. Udall Secretary of the *Interior*.

Bob Hope was honored at a dinner in Hollywood for his outstanding work in entertaining American servicemen overseas. One of the highlights of the dinner was the tape recorded voice of President Kennedy. The President lauded Mr. Hope for his humanitarian efforts and suggested that Mr. Hope consider a Road-to-Washington picture:

From my own experience, I can tell him it's not the easiest road to travel, but it will give him a chance to visit his money—at least what's left of it.

March 4, 1962

Washington is a city of Southern efficiency and Northern charm.

Quoted by William Manchester in "Portrait of a President"

At a Washington dinner party shortly after his inauguration, President Kennedy paid tribute to Washington lawyer Clark Clifford, who had served as Mr. Kennedy's representative to the Eisenhower administration during the period of transition immediately after Mr. Kennedy's election:

Clark is a wonderful fellow. In a day when so many are seeking a reward for what they contributed to the return of the Democrats to the White House, you don't hear Clark clamoring. He was invaluable to us and all he asked in return was that we advertise his law firm on the backs of one dollar bills.

February, 1961

Barry Goldwater is an excellent photographer. He once took a good picture of President Kennedy and sent it to him for an autograph. The picture came back with this inscription:

For Barry Goldwater, whom I urge to follow the career for which he has shown so much talent—photography. From his friend, John Kennedy.

It would be premature to ask your support in the next election and it would be inaccurate to thank you for it in the past.

National Industrial Conference Board
Washington, D. C.
February 13, 1961

I appreciate very much your generous invitation to be here tonight.

You bear heavy responsibilities these days and an article I read some time ago reminded me of how particularly heavy the burdens of present-day events bear upon your profession.

You may remember that in 1851, the *New York Herald Tribune*, under the sponsorship of Horace Greeley, included as its London correspondent an obscure journalist by the name of Karl Marx.

We are told that the foreign correspondent, Marx, stone broke and with a family ill and undernourished, constantly appealed to Greeley and managing editor Charles Dana for an increase in his munificent salary of $5 per installment, a salary which he and Engels labelled as the "lousiest petty bourgeois cheating."

But when all his financial appeals were refused, Marx looked around for other means of livelihood and fame, and eventually terminated his relationship with the *Tribune* and devoted his talents full time to the cause that would bequeath to the world the seeds of Leninism, Stalinism, revolution and the Cold War.

If only this capitalistic New York newspaper had treated him more kindly, if only Marx had remained a foreign correspondent, history might have been different, and I hope all publishers will bear this lesson in mind the next time they receive a poverty-stricken appeal for a small increase in the expense account from an obscure newspaperman.

I have selected as the title of my remarks tonight "The President and the Press." Some may suggest that this would be more naturally worded "The President vs. the Press," but these are not my sentiments tonight.

It is true, however, that when a well-known diplomat from another country demanded recently that our State Department repudiate certain newspaper attacks on his colleague, it was necessary for us to reply that this Administration was not responsible for the press, for the press had already made it clear that it was not responsible for this administration.

If in the last few months, your White House reporters and photographers have been attending church services with regularity that has surely done them no harm.

On the other hand, I realize that your staff and wire service photographers may be complaining that they do not enjoy the same green privileges at the local golf courses which they once did. It is true that my predecessor did not object as I do to pictures of one's golfing skill in action. But neither, on the other hand, did he ever bean a Secret Service man.

American Newspaper Publishers Association
April 27, 1961

I also regret very much that another honored guest of this dinner on a previous occasion is not with us tonight. I follow his career with more interest than he might imagine. In his quest for the Presidency, Governor Rockefeller follows the examples of other distinguished New Yorkers—Wendell Willkie, Thomas Dewey, Richard Nixon—and I wish him some margin of success.

Protestant Council of New York
November 8, 1963

On a return visit to the White House, former President Truman entertained President Kennedy and the assembled dinner guests with a few selections on the piano. President Kennedy was quoted as having made this comment after Mr. Truman finished his piano recital:

Don't say there is no justice in the world. Stalin has been kicked out of Lenin's tomb and President Truman is back in the White House.

November 5, 1961

There is no city in the United States in which I get a warmer welcome and less votes than Columbus, Ohio.

January 6, 1962

I used to work for INS for a short time, although I have never been able to figure out whether UP belongs to INS or INS belongs to UP.

I want to say that I come here not as a stranger, because I have had during my first five months in office the close observation of Mr. Merriman Smith [UPI White House correspondent], who carried other Presidents through difficult periods before, and who is regarded as one of the leading Presidential collectors of our time.

United Press International Dinner
June 9, 1961

I want to say that I have been in on-the-job training for about eleven months and feel that I have some seniority rights.

I am delighted to be here with you and with the Secretary of Labor, Arthur Goldberg. I was up in New York, stressing physical fitness, and in line with that, Arthur went over with a group to Switzerland to climb some of the mountains there. They got up about five and he was in bed. He got up to join them later and when they all came back at four o'clock in the afternoon he didn't come back with them.

So they sent out search parties and there was not a sign that afternoon and night. The next day the Red Cross went out and around, calling: "Goldberg, Goldberg! It's the Red Cross!" Then this voice came down from the mountain: "I gave at the office!"

Those are the liberties you can take with members of the cabinet.

AFL-CIO Convention
Bal Harbour, Florida
December 7, 1961

Let me begin by expressing my appreciation for the very deep honor you have conferred upon me. As General de Gaulle occasionally acknowledges America to be the daughter of Europe, so I am pleased to come to Yale, the daughter of Harvard.

It might be said now that I have the best of both worlds: a Harvard education and a Yale degree.

I am particularly glad to become a Yale man because as I think about my troubles, I find that a lot of

them have come from other Yale men. Among businessmen, I have had a minor disagreement with Roger Blough of the Law School Class of 1931 and I have had some complaints too from my friend, Henry Luce, of the class of 1920, not to mention, always, William F. Buckley, Jr., of the class of 1950.

Yale Commencement Address
June 11, 1962

I would like to announce at this time that as Commander-in-Chief, I am exercising my privilege of directing the Secretary of the Army and the Superintendent of West Point to remit all existing confinements and other cadet punishments and I hope it will be possible to carry this out today.

General Westmoreland was slightly pained to hear that this was impending in view of the fact that one cadet, who I am confident will some day be head of the Army, had just been committed for eight months and is about to be released. But I am glad to have this opportunity to participate in the advancement of his military career.

I want to say that I wish all of you the greatest success. While I say that, I am not unmindful of the fact that two graduates of this Academy have reached the White House and neither was a member of my party. Until I'm more certain that this trend will be broken, I wish that all of you may be generals and not Commanders-in-Chief.

West Point Commencement Address
June 7, 1962

President Kennedy, in the very early days of his administration, was always cognizant of the fact that many of the situations he faced were a result of actions of the previous administration. At an early meeting of the National Security Council, President Kennedy opened a folder filled with briefs of US problems: "Now, let's see," the President said, "Did we inherit these or are these our own?"

On the same subject, President Kennedy had this to say: "I had plenty of problems when I came in, but wait until the fellow that follows me sees what he will inherit."

There are not so many differences between politics and football. Some Republicans have been unkind enough to suggest that my close election was somewhat similar to the Notre Dame—Syracuse game [won by Notre Dame with a disputed penalty]. But I am like Notre Dame. We just take it as it comes along. We're not giving it back.

Politics is an astonishing profession. It has enabled me to go from being an obscure member of the junior varsity at Harvard to being an honorary member of the Football Hall of Fame.

> *National Football Foundation Dinner*
> *New York City*
> *December, 1961*

After President Kennedy had nominated John Galbraith as the new United States Ambassador to India, Mr. Kennedy was informed by Mr. Galbraith that the Ambassador-to-be's young son, Peter, was not too anxious

to leave all his friends in Boston and move to India. The President sent the following soothing letter to young Peter Galbraith:

Dear Peter:

I learned from your father that you are not anxious to give up your school and friends for India.

I think I know a little bit about how you feel.

More than 20 years ago, our family was similarly uprooted when we went to London where my father was Ambassador.

My younger brother and sisters were about your age. They had, like you, to exchange new friends for old.

For anyone interested, as your father says you are, in animals, India has the most fascinating possibilities. The range is from elephants to cobras, although I gather the cobras have to be handled professionally.

As a P.S. the President added:

I wish a little I were going also.

April 1, 1961

The following note was sent by President Kennedy to Prime Minister Diefenbaker of Canada after Mr. Diefenbaker had expressed his regrets over the fact that President Kennedy had sprained his back in a tree-planting ceremony on the President's recent visit to Canada.

Many thanks for your gracious message. The tree will be there long after the discomfort is gone.

June 9, 1961

Prior to his becoming President, John F. Kennedy was a member of the Harvard Board of Overseers. President Kennedy attended his last meeting as a member of the Harvard Board of Overseers immediately after his election. As he entered University Hall to attend that last meeting, he was met by cheering students. The new President turned to the students and said:

I am here to go over your grades with Dr. Pusey and I'll protect your interests.

January 9, 1961

I think this is the most extraordinary collection of talent, of human knowledge, that has ever been gathered together at the White House—with the possible exception of when Thomas Jefferson dined alone.

*White House dinner
honoring Nobel Prize winners*

In a note to Arthur Hays Sulzberger, chairman of the Board of The New York Times, *Mr. Kennedy had this to say concerning Mr. Sulzberger's recent acquisition of a new rocking chair:*

You will recall what Senator Dirksen said about the rocking chair—it gives you a sense of motion without any sense of danger.

May 1, 1961

I recognize tonight that I bear a heavy responsibility of having kept a distinguished group of Americans who paid $125 for this dinner from that dinner for an hour and thirty minutes.

But, I will say that—if I may quote an old East Side expression—what you have lost on bananas, you are going to make up on the apples, because this could have been one of the longest dinners in the history of these occasions.

Lyndon [Johnson] is good for forty-five minutes, when he is given a chance; Ambassador Stevenson has been known to go for a very long time; Frank Pace has a very long story to tell; and Bob Hope, will, if called upon. So this might have gone to one or two in the morning but, because of my imminent journey to Paris, you'll be out—hungry, rather unhappy—but you will be home early tonight.

It is now one-thirty in Paris and I am due there at ten-thirty, and I do not believe it would be a good start to keep the General waiting. So I shall be brief. . . .

Eleanor Roosevelt Cancer Foundation Dinner
New York City
May 30, 1961

Those of you who regard my profession of political life with some disdain should remember that it made it possible for me to move from being an obscure lieutenant in the United States Navy to Commander-in-Chief in fourteen years with very little technical competence.

University of North Carolina
October 12, 1961

In a campaign speech for Richard J. Hughes in his race for the New Jersey Governorship against former Secretary of Labor James P. Mitchell, President Kennedy had this to say:

One year ago at this time I came to this city around dark after having made about fifteen speeches. In the last nine months, I'm happy to say this is the first stump speech I've made for a candidate and I'm glad it's here in New Jersey.

I am somewhat out of practice. But I will say that the last time I came to New Jersey it was just after Mr. Nixon had turned down the fifth debate. And I gather that Mr. Mitchell feels that no Republican should ever be caught in debate again.

November 2, 1961

Secretary of Labor Arthur Goldberg was credited with averting a strike at the Metropolitan Opera during 1961. President Kennedy paid notice to Mr. Goldberg's efforts at a Washington dinner party where the entertainment included Metropolitan Opera stars Roberta Peters and Jerome Hines. In introducing the opera stars to the audience, the President remarked:

The singers have appeared here under the sponsorship of Arthur Goldberg.

September 25, 1961

For all I have been reading in the last three, four or five months about the great conservative revival sweeping the United States, I thought perhaps no one was going to show up today.

Young Democrats Convention
Miami Beach, Florida
December, 1961

A few years ago it was said that the optimists learned Russian and the pessimists learned Chinese. I prefer to think that those with vision study French and English.

Paris, France
June 1, 1961

Theodore C. Sorensen was a key Kennedy aide and chief speechwriter for the President. Rarely did Mr. Sorensen make any speeches of his own. However, Mr. Sorensen did make one speech in Nebraska in which he criticized their educational system. This speech by Mr. Sorensen had many Nebraskans up in arms. When asked about the predicament that Mr. Sorensen found himself in, Mr. Kennedy remarked:

That's what happens when you let a speechwriter out on his own.

July, 1961

President Kennedy enlivened the ceremony for signing of a housing bill with a touch of Shakespeare. Noting the absence of two Alabama Democrats, Representative Albert Rains and Senator John J. Sparkman, who had maneuvered the bill through Congress, the President declared:

Having this bill signed without them here is somewhat like having *Hamlet* played without the Prince.

Washington, D. C. July 2, 1961

The last time that I came to this stadium was twenty-two years ago, when I visited it in November of 1940 as a student at a near-by small school for the game with Stanford. I must say, I had a much warmer reception today than I did on that occasion. In those days, we used to fill these universities for football, and now we do it for academic events, and I'm not sure that this doesn't represent a rather dangerous trend for the future of our country.

University of California
March 23, 1962

It has recently been suggested that whether I serve one or two terms in the Presidency, I will find myself at the end of that period at what might be called the awkward age, too old to begin a new career and too young to write my memoirs.

National Industrial Conference Board
Washington, D. C. February 13, 1961

Poet Robert Frost was honored by Congress. The noted poet was presented the Congressional Medal in recognition of his contributions to American letters. In awarding the medal to Mr. Frost at the White House, President Kennedy said that he supposed that the poet was disappointed that it was not a more controversial decision by Congress in voting the medal for Mr. Frost but a unanimous one. The President went on to say:

It's the only thing they've been able to agree on for a long time.

March 25, 1961

When we got into office, the thing that surprised me most was to find that things were just as bad as we'd been saying they were.

Washington, D. C. Dinner honoring President Kennedy's 44th birthday May 27, 1961

The President made this response to a group of women delegates to the United Nations who had suggested at a White House function that someday there might be a woman President:

I want to say that I had not expected that the standard of revolt would be raised in the Royal Pavilion here, but I'm always rather nervous about how you talk about women who are active in politics, whether they want to be talked about as women or as politicians.

I am delighted to learn of the testimonial luncheon. I know that the Postmaster General will enjoy his day off in Springfield, and I am only sorry that I cannot join in this tribute.

I am sending this message by wire, since I want to be certain that this message reaches you in the right place and at the right time.

> *Reply to an invitation to attend testimonial luncheon in honor of the then Postmaster General Edward Day in Springfield, Illinois*

This is a double birthday party today. The Children's Bureau is fifty years old and so is Secretary Ribicoff. This is an awkward birthday for the Secretary, because he is too young to retire and too old to be President.

> *Fiftieth Anniversary of the United States Children's Bureau Washington, D. C. April 8, 1962*

I feel at home here because I number in my own state of Massachusetts many friends and former constituents who are of Canadian descent. Their vote is enough to determine the outcome of an election, even a Presidential election. You can understand that having been elected President of the United States by less than 140 thousand votes out of 60 million, that I am very conscious of these statistics.

Introducing Astronaut Alan Shepard, Jr.:

We have with us today the nation's number one television performer, who I think on last Friday morning secured the largest rating of any morning show in recent history.

And I think it does credit to him that he is associated with such a distinguished group of Americans whom we are all glad to honor today—his companions in the flight to outer space—so I think we'll give them all a hand. They are the tanned and healthy ones; the others are Washington employees.

I also want to pay a particular tribute to some of the people who worked in this flight; Robert Gilruth, who was director of the Space Task Force Group at Langley Field; Walter Williams, the operations director of Project Mercury; the NASA Deputy Administrator, Dr. Hugh Dryden; Lieutenant Colonel Glenn, Jr. and, of course, Jim Webb, who is head of NASA.

Most of these names are unfamiliar. If the flight had not been an overwhelming success, these names would be very familiar to everyone.

*Washington Ceremony honoring
Astronaut Alan Shepard, Jr.
May 8, 1961*

My experience in government is that when things are non-controversial, beautifully coordinated and all the rest, it must be that there is not much going on.

Whenever he addressed a meeting of the National Association of Manufacturers, President Kennedy was cognizant of the fact that he was not speaking before the friendliest of audiences. Mr. Kennedy opened an address to the NAM in December, 1961 with these remarks:

I understand that President McKinley and I are the only two Presidents of the United States to ever address such an occasion. I suppose that President McKinley and I are the only two that are regarded as fiscally sound enough to be qualified for admission to this organization on an occasion such as this.

Special ceremonies were held at the White House in November, 1961 in honor of the 46th biennial general assembly of the Union of American Hebrew Congregations. At these ceremonies President Kennedy received a gift of a Sacred Torah. In accepting the Torah, the President turned to the then Secretary of Labor, Arthur Goldberg, who is a trustee of the Union of American Hebrew Congregations, and said:

I'll ask the Secretary of Labor to translate this for me.

Some years ago, in the city of Fall River, Massachusetts, the Mayor was elected by one vote, and every time he went down the street, everyone would come up to him and say, "Say, Dan, I put you in office."

And I feel a little like that in Chicago tonight. If all of you had voted the other way—there's about fifty-five hundred of you here tonight—I wouldn't be President of the United States.

I am delighted that John Bailey's going to take over this job [Chairman of the Democratic National Committee]. He is more popular today than he will be any time again in his life. I will feel that he is doing a good job when you all say, "Well, Kennedy is all right, but Bailey's the one who is really making the mistakes."

Those of us who had difficulty navigating at sea are astonished at the ability to navigate under ice.

White House ceremony honoring submarine and Arctic research scientist Waldo K. Lyon August 7, 1962

Last year, more Americans went to symphonies than went to baseball games. This may be viewed as an alarming statistic, but I think that both baseball and the country will endure.

White House Youth Concert August 6, 1962

It's a vital business, the running of a democracy, and it's important that all of us register and vote for the party of our choice.

I am supporting the party of my choice and I intend to vote in the November elections.

Washington, D. C.
August 28, 1962

I feel honored to join you at this distinguished university.

In the year 1717, King George I of England donated a very valuable library to Cambridge University and at very nearly the same time, had occasion to dispatch a regiment to Oxford.

The King, remarked one famous wit, had judiciously observed the condition of both universities—one was a learned body in need of loyalty and the other was a loyal body in need of learning.

I am deeply honored by the degree which you awarded me today and I think it is appropriate to speak at this university noted for both loyalty and learning.

University of Maine
October 19, 1963

The only other President to have visited Ashland was Calvin Coolidge, who never said a word. I was here for only one night and spoke all the time.

Ashland, Wisconsin
September 24, 1963

In September, 1963, at the Salt Lake City, Utah, airport, President Kennedy pulled the switch to activate generators at the Green River in the Colorado River basin 150 miles away.

I never know when I press these whether I am going to blow up Massachusetts or start the project.

Then the President listened intently to the loudspeaker for the voice that was supposed to announce the successful starting of the generators.

If we don't hear from him, it's back to the drawing boards.

While most segments of the economy are producing more with fewer men than before, Chicago is an exception to the pattern, since it now takes ten men to manage the Chicago Cubs instead of one.

Dedication of O'Hare International Airport, Chicago, Illinois March 24, 1963

Karl Marx used to write for the *Herald Tribune*, but that isn't why I cancelled my subscription.

November 18, 1962

Last week, after speaking to the Chamber of Commerce and the AMA, I began to wonder how I got elected and now I remember . . . .

I flew longer—and this will go down in the history books—I flew longer in a helicopter than any President of the United States to come here today. That's the kind of forward looking administration we have.

United Auto Workers Convention
Atlantic City, New Jersey
May 8, 1962

I'm very proud to be here tonight. I'm particularly interested in the fact that two of our distinguished guests are former Prime Ministers of Peru and are now publishers of newspapers.

It does suggest to those who hold office that when the time comes that if, as they say in the United States, if you can't beat them, join them.

Inter-American Press Association
Miami Beach, Florida
November 18, 1963

Greeting students who had been learning about government as participants in the Senate youth program, on February 1, 1963, President Kennedy expressed the hope that one of the young men in the group would one day occupy the White House—but not right away!

The other day I read in a newspaper where Senator Goldwater asked for labor's support before 2,000 cheering Illinois businessmen . . . .

Three years ago and one week, by a landslide, the people of the United States elected me to the Presidency of this country.

> *AFL-CIO Convention*
> *New York City*
> *November 15, 1963*

I used to wonder when I was in the House how President Truman got into so much trouble. Now I'm beginning to get the idea . . . .

I'm sorry to see Matt go. He's the only businessman we have left.

> *Washington dinner honoring*
> *Matthew McClosky, former Democratic*
> *National Treasurer*
> *Mayflower Hotel, June 10, 1962*

Sometimes I wish I just had a summer job here.

> *To students working in Washington*
> *June 21, 1962*

Waterbury is either the easiest city to get crowds or it has the best Democrats in the United States.

> *Waterbury, Connecticut*
> *October 11, 1962*

I want to express my appreciation for becoming an instant graduate of this academy and I consider it an honor.

I congratulate you all, and most of all, I congratulate your mothers and fathers who made it possible.

> *United States Air Force Academy*
> *Graduation Exercises in Colorado Springs*
> *June 5, 1963*

I want to register an official protest with the International Ladies' Garment Workers of the sweatshop conditions under which we are working today. I'm not sure that this represents fifty years of progress. It is true that your distinguished President [David Dubinsky] invited me to come to speak on November 3rd as we were heading to a meeting which he was sponsoring three days before election. I would have agreed to anything.

> *I.L.G.W.U. Housing Project, New York City*
> *May 19, 1962*

One Las Vegas gambler is supposed to have said he hoped we'd be as tough on Berlin as we've been on Las Vegas. Well, we intend to be.

> *U. S. Attorneys Meeting*
> *White House, October 10, 1962*

THE FAMILY

THE FAMILY

"I do not think it entirely inappropriate to introduce myself to this audience. I am the man who accompanied Jacqueline Kennedy to Paris, and I have enjoyed it.

SHAPE Headquarters
Paris, France
June 2, 1961

Ever since his brother began to serve as his campaign manager, the President had been receiving advice from seasoned politicians who considered Robert Kennedy too young for such a big job. The President had this to say to a group of worried Democratic leaders prior to the 1960 campaign:

If I need somebody older, there's no need to go outside of the family. I can always get my Father.

I want you to meet my sister, Patricia Lawford, from California. Somebody asked her last week if I was her kid brother, so she knew it was time this campaign came to an end.

Manchester, New Hampshire
November 7, 1960

I see nothing wrong with giving Robert some legal experience as Attorney General before he goes out to practice law.

Alfa Club
Washington, D. C.
January 21, 1961

On this matter of experience, I had announced earlier this year that if successful I would not consider campaign contributions as a substitute for experience in appointing Ambassadors. Ever since I made that statement I have not received one single cent from my Father.

Alfred E. Smith Memorial Dinner
New York City
October 19, 1960

The President went on to quip about his wife's recent trip to India.

I know my Republican friends were glad to see my wife feeding an elephant in India. She gave him sugar and nuts. But, of course, the elephant wasn't satisfied.

President Kennedy made these remarks at a dinner of the Gridiron Club. Referring to his sister-in-law, Princess Radziwill, President Kennedy said:

It is not true that we're going to change the name of Lafayette Square to Radziwill Square—at least, not during my first term.

The President made reference to his efforts to convince Americans to drink milk.

I am certainly enjoying being with you newsmen this evening. None of you know how tough it is to have to drink milk three times a day.

Washington, D. C.
February, 1962

Attorney General Robert F. Kennedy got into hot water with the state of Texas when he remarked that the war with Mexico was not a very bright page in the history of the United States. Shortly after making that remark, the Attorney General was asked if he had anything further to say about the Mexican War. Mr. Kennedy replied that he'd spoken to the President about the matter and that the President said he wasn't "going to muzzle me," but from now on all speeches on Texas should be cleared with the Vice President.

March 4, 1962

I have just received the following telegram from my generous Daddy. It says, "Dear Jack: Don't buy a single vote more than is necessary. I'll be damned if I'm going to pay for a landslide."

Gridiron Dinner
Washington, D. C.
1958

In the last campaign most of the members of this luncheon group today supported my opponent—except for a very few who were under the impression that I was my father's son.

National Association of
Manufacturers
December 6, 1961

I have been presented with this donkey by two young ladies down there for my daughter. My daughter has the greatest collection of donkeys. She doesn't even know what an elephant looks like. We are going to protect her from that knowledge.

I come here to Florida today where my family has lived for thirty years, where they have already voted for one of the two candidates, and I feel it looks pretty good to get at least two votes in Florida.

Miami, Florida
October 18, 1960

Ladies and gentlemen, Paul Douglas, the present U. S. Senator and the next U. S. Senator, Hayes Beall, candidate for the Congress from this district, and my sister, Eunice, Mrs. Sargent Shriver, who lives in Illinois. One of my sisters is married to someone who lives in New York, one in California. We realized long ago we have to carry New York, Illinois and California.

Elgin, Illinois
October 25, 1960

I want to express my great appreciation at the opportunity to be here with you, and to express my thanks to all of you for having attended this [Youth Fitness] Conference. I asked those members of the Cabinet who felt they were physically fit to come here today and I am delighted that Mr. Udall and Mr. Robert Kennedy and Governor Ribicoff responded to the challenge.

Question: Mr. President, the people of Florida are hoping that you and your family will again spend Christmas with them. Can you tell us what your present plans are, sir?

President Kennedy: My Mother and Father are going to Florida in December and my wife and children hope to be there for Christmas and if my situation permits, I will go at Christmas. If the question is the result of some stories that the tourist business in Florida is off because of our difficulties, I do not think it will be.

November 20, 1962

Question: Mr. President, it has been a long time since a President and his family have been subjected to such a heavy barrage of teasing and fun-poking and satire .There have been books on Backstairs at the White House and cartoon books with clever sayings and photo albums with balloons and now there is a smash hit record. Can you tell us whether you read them and listened to them and whether they produced annoyment or enjoyment?

President Kennedy: Annoyment. Yes, I have read them and listened to Mr. Meader's record, but I thought it sounded more like Teddy than it did me, so he's annoyed.

I will introduce myself. I am Teddy Kennedy's brother, and I'm glad to be here tonight.

> *Democratic Rally, Harrisburg, Pennsylvania*
> *September 20, 1962*

I want you to know that we are very grateful to all of you . . . to Jack Benny who came to help an older man.

I don't know whether you realize that this is an historic occasion. We have paid off nearly $4,000,000 that the Kennedy-Johnson ticket ran up in November of 1960. It is now gone forever, which is sad, and all we have left is the Federal deficit.

I would like to recall a speech which Franklin Roosevelt made in regard to his dog. He said, "these Republican leaders have not been content with attacks on me, or my wife or my brothers, no not content with that, they now include my little girl's pony, Macaroni." Well, I don't resent such attacks but Macaroni does.

Actually, there is another speech by a former Vice-President of the United States in 1952 which is even more pertinent.

It was just a little pony and you know, the kids, like all kids, loved it. And I just want to say this right now: that regardless of what they say about it, we're going to keep it. I feel about Macaroni like the Vice President did about Checkers. We're just going to go ahead.

I got a telegram tonight which said, "in honor of your birthday, I believe that you should get a rise in pay."

Signed "Roger"
[*Roger Blough, President of United States Steel*]

"P.S. My birthday is next month."

At four o'clock tomorrow, we're going to have a rally here on Medical Care for the Aged. Those who would prefer to stay and wait will find us all back here at the same stand. And in the meanwhile, let me tell you what a pleasure it is once in a while to get out of Washington and not read the papers but come and see the voters.

New York's Birthday Salute to President Kennedy
Madison Square Garden, May 19, 1962

During the hard-fought and crucial West Virginia primary, President Kennedy's youngest brother, Ted, had just finished giving an enthusiastic speech in which he had said, "Do you want a man who will give the country leadership? Do you want a man who has vigor and vision?" When candidate Jack Kennedy took the microphone from his young brother, he opened his remarks by saying:

I would like to tell my brother that you cannot be elected President until you are thirty-five years of age.

THE PRESS CONFERENCES

THE PRESS CONFERENCES

President Kennedy was asked to comment on the press treatment of his administration thus far:

Well, I'm reading more and enjoying it less.

May 9, 1962

At a press conference in February of 1961, a reporter asked Mr. Kennedy what steps the Government was considering to stop Cuban exports to this country. He specifically mentioned the shipment of molasses. After discussing the general problem, the President turned to the subject of molasses. He paused for a moment and said:

I believe it's going to be made into gin—and I'm not sure that's in the public interest.

President Kennedy was asked to comment about the election of Mayor Robert F. Wagner of New York and Governor Hughes of New Jersey. The reporters wanted to know if the President felt that since both Mayor Wagner and Governor Hughes were Democrats that their election indicated that things looked good for the Democrats in future elections.

They won because they were effective candidates. But they ran as Democrats. And I believe that it indicates that the American people believe that the candidates and parties in those areas, as well as nationally, are committed to progress. So I am happy, and I suppose some day we will lose and then I'll have to eat those words.

November, 1961

Question: Mr. President, you have said, and I think more than once, that heads of government should not go to the summit to negotiate agreements but only to approve agreements negotiated at a lower level. Now it's being said and written that you're going to eat those words and go to a summit without any agreement at a lower level. Has your position changed, sir?

President Kennedy: Well, I'm going to have a dinner for all the people who've written it and we'll see who eats what.

March 7, 1962

It was during a Presidential Press Conference that President Kennedy received the news that the United States had successfully launched a chimpanzee into space. The President interrupted the press conference to announce the event to the assembled reporters:

This chimpanzee who was flying in space took off at 10:08. He reports that everything is going perfectly and working well.

November 29, 1961

Question: Mr. President, some time ago you said that you were reading more now but enjoying it less. Do you have any more current observations on American journalism or on your personal reading habits?

President Kennedy: No, I want to say that I am looking forward to all of you coming to the White House this afternoon between six and seven. Mr. Arthur Krock wrote of the temptations and seductions which take place in the press in the White House. But I want you to know that we expect that you will all emerge with your journalistic integrity and virtue unmarred. You will be courteous to the host on all occasions but it is not necessary that your views be changed.

American Society of Newspaper Editors, Washington, D. C. April 19, 1963

Question: There have been published reports that some high-placed Republican people have been making overtures to your Secretary of Defense for him to be their 1968 candidate for President. If you thought that Mr. McNamara were seriously considering these overtures, would you continue him in your cabinet?

President Kennedy: I have too high a regard for him to launch his candidacy yet.

January 25, 1963

Question: Mr. President, now that the United States is being transmitted instantaneously overseas via Tel star, do you think the U.S. networks should make a greater effort to do something about the "vast wasteland"?

President Kennedy: I'm going to leave Mr. Minow to argue the wasteland issue, I think.

July 24, 1962

Question: The Republican National Committee recently adopted a resolution saying you were pretty much of a failure. How do you feel about that?

President Kennedy: I assume it passed unanimously.

July 17, 1963

Question: Mr. President, Senator Margaret Chase Smith has proposed that a watchdog committee be created. What is your reaction?

President Kennedy: To watch Congressmen and Senators? Well, that will be fine if they feel they should be watched.

March 21, 1963